Letters to My Son

Living as a Man After God's Own Heart

Amy Tisdale

KINGDOM REIGN PUBLISHING

Letters to My Son: Living as a Man After God's Own Heart

Copyright© 2025 by Amy Tisdale

All rights reserved.

No part of this publication may be reproduced, stored in a retrieval system, or transmitted in any form or by any means—electronic, mechanical, photocopying, recording, or otherwise—without the prior written permission of the author, except in the case of brief quotations embodied in critical articles or reviews. This book is a work of personal encouragement and biblical reflection. It is not intended to replace professional counseling, discipleship, or pastoral guidance.

Scripture quotations are taken from the Holy Bible, New International Version® (NIV®), unless otherwise noted. Copyright © 1973, 1978, 1984, 2011 by Biblica, Inc.™ Used by permission. All rights reserved worldwide.

Cover Art by Amy Tisdale

Cover and book formatting by Kingdom Reign Publishing.

https://travisandtiffanytombre.com/kingdomreignpublishing/

Printed in the United States of America

ISBN: 979-8-9987905-1-5

First Edition: 2025

For more from the author, visit: authoredbyamy.net

Contents

Dedication		V
Introduction		VII
1.	Letter 1 Knowing Who You Are in Christ	1
2.	Letter 2 When You Face Doubt	3
3.	Letter 3 Don't Forget Where You Came From	4
4.	Letter 4 Trusting God When It's Hard	6
5.	Letter 5 Choosing Friends Wisely	8
6.	Letter 6 Guarding Your Heart	11
7.	Letter 7 Integrity in the Small Things	14
8.	Letter 8 Living with Purpose	17

9.	Letter 9	20
	Becoming a Man of Prayer	
10.	Letter 10	23
	Courage to Stand Alone	
11.	Letter 11	26
	When You Fall Short —Grace After Failure	
12.	Letter 12	28
	Handling Temptation and Choosing What's Right	
13.	Letter 13	31
	Stewardship—Money, Time, and Responsibility	
14.	Letter 14	34
	Honoring Women and Building Godly Relationships	
15.	Letter 15	37
	Living as a Servant Leader	
16.	Letter 16	39
	Finding Your Identity in a World That Labels You	
17.	Letter 17	42
	Choosing Humility Over Pride	
18.	Letter 18	45
	Dealing with Disappointment and Delayed Dreams	
19.	Letter 19	48
	Being a Light in a Dark World	
20.	Letter 20	51
	Living for an Audience of One	
21.	Final Blessing and Prayer	54
About the author		56
Amy Tisdale		

Dedication

To my son, Caleb —
  my greatest earthly gift and one of the brightest lights in my life!
  These letters are for you —
  to guide you, encourage you, and remind you of who you are
  and the God who made you. I love you so very much!
  May you always walk boldly in truth,
  stand firmly in grace and live every day knowing how deeply you are loved.
  I am proud of the man you are becoming
  and humbled to be your mom.
  With all my heart,
  Mom

Introduction

Dear Caleb,

From the moment I found out I was going to be your mom; I started praying for the man you would become. Not just for your grades, your talents, or your future career—but for your heart as well. I prayed you would love Jesus more than anything else. I prayed you would be kind, honest, steady, and strong in the ways that truly matter. And I prayed that you would walk through this world with your head held high, not because of your accomplishments, but because you know Whose you are.

This book is a collection of letters written from that place—a mother's heart full of love, truth, and deep hope for her son. These words aren't just advice for the road ahead. They are reminders of who you are, what matters most, and how to live as a man after God's own heart in a world that will try to pull you in every direction but the right one.

You will face joys and challenges, victories and valleys. You will have days when you feel invincible and others when you feel completely lost. But through it all, I want you to have something solid to return to. These letters are meant to be a steady voice, reminding you of the things I hope you never forget—that your identity is found in Christ, that prayer changes everything, that integrity matters, that you were created for a purpose, and that sometimes the bravest thing you can do is stand alone.

This isn't a rulebook. It's not a manual. It's my heart, in print, for you. And if there's one thing I hope you remember above all else, it's this: You are deeply loved. By me. And even more so, by the God who made you.

Always remember Whose you are and Who you represent.
I love you always, no matter what,
Mom

Letter 1

Knowing Who You Are in Christ

Dear Caleb,

The world will constantly try to define you. It will offer you labels based on your performance, appearance, relationships, and even your failures. But I want you to remember something that will never change: You are who God says you are. You are chosen, redeemed, loved, and created with intentionality (Ephesians 1:4-5, NIV).

There is no mistake in you. The Creator of the universe knew exactly what He was doing when He made you. As life unfolds, your identity will be tested. You might be tempted to chase approval, to mold yourself into what others expect, or to question your value. But Caleb, don't let your worth hang on the opinions of the world. People's opinions shift like sand, but God's truth is a solid rock. He calls you His child (John 1:12, NIV), His workmanship (Ephesians 2:10, NIV), and a royal priesthood (1 Peter 2:9, NIV).

When you feel lost, turn to the Word. When you feel unseen, turn to the cross. When you feel uncertain, remember the empty tomb. God's love for you is not based on what you do but on who He is. Walk confidently in your identity—not in pride, but in purpose. You're not just a good man. You are a godly man in the making.

Remember Whose you are and Who you represent.
And don't forget to call your mom. ;)

Letter 2

When You Face Doubt

Dear Caleb,

There will be moments when faith feels fragile—when prayers seem to bounce off the ceiling and your heart carries more questions than answers. I need you to know doubt is not the enemy of faith. It's often the soil where deeper faith grows.

Think about Thomas, the disciple known for his doubt. Jesus didn't shame him. He invited Thomas to touch His wounds and see for himself (John 20:27, NIV). That's the heart of our Savior. He welcomes questions when they come with a heart that's still seeking Him. Doubt means you're thinking. Wrestling. Wanting more of God, not less. And He honors that. James 1:5 (NIV) promises, "If any of you lacks wisdom, you should ask God, who gives generously to all without finding fault."

Ask the questions, Caleb. Dig deep. Surround yourself with believers who won't give you easy answers, but who will walk with you through the hard ones. Don't let your doubt isolate you. Let it lead you to the One who never leaves you. Faith isn't the absence of questions—it's the decision to trust God in the middle of them.

Remember Whose you are and Who you represent.
Today would be a good day to send your mom a selfie. ;)

Letter 3

Don't Forget Where You Came From

Dear Caleb,

As you launch into this new season of life, everything will feel fresh: new classes, new people, new ideas, new freedom. It's easy to get caught up in excitement and lose touch with your roots. But I pray you always carry them with you. You come from a home built on grace. You've seen God move in quiet ways and powerful ones. You've sat through family devotions, laughed around the dinner table, and prayed when life got messy. None of that was accidental. Those were seeds planted in your heart.

Deuteronomy 6:6-7 (NIV) says, "These commandments that I give you today are to be on your hearts. Impress them on your children. Talk about them when you sit at home and when you walk along the road, when you lie down and when you get up." That's what we've tried to do.

So, as you make choices, as you form convictions, as you grow into the man God created you to be—remember where you came from. Remember the stories, the prayers, the laughter, and even the tears. They shaped you. And they'll steady you when things feel uncertain.

And Caleb, if you ever forget, come home. There's always a seat at our table.

Remember Whose you are and Who you represent.
Today you should text your mom and tell her what she means to you ;)

Letter 4

Trusting God When It's Hard

Dear Caleb,

Life won't always make sense. You'll face situations that stretch you, break you, and leave you questioning how anything good could come from the mess. I know, because I've lived it. But I need you to know—especially in those moments—God is still with you. Romans 8:28 (NIV) says, "And we know that in all things God works for the good of those who love him, who have been called according to his purpose." That doesn't mean everything will feel good. It means God wastes nothing.

When I had my stroke, nothing about it felt good. It was terrifying. Painful. Life altering. But God never stepped off the throne. He never left. And as hard as it's been, I've seen His goodness even in the valley. I've felt His nearness through your dad's love, through the prayers of friends, and through the strength He gives me to wake up and keep going.

You'll have your own valleys, Caleb. Maybe different from mine, but valleys, nonetheless. In those times, don't run from God—run to Him. Don't try to understand everything. Trust the One who does. He's writing a bigger story than what you see in the moment. His timing is perfect. His grace is sufficient. And His love never fails.

Hold tight to Him when everything else feels like it's falling apart. Trusting God doesn't mean you'll always feel strong. It means you know where your strength comes from.

Remember Whose you are and Who you represent.
And don't forget to call your mom. ;)

Letter 5

Choosing Friends Wisely

Dear Caleb,

I've told you this since you were little, and I'll say it again now: your friends will shape your future more than almost anything else in your life.

The people you choose to surround yourself with will either help you grow into the man God has created you to be, or they will slowly pull you away from that purpose—sometimes without you even noticing. Proverbs 13:20 (NIV) says, "Walk with the wise and become wise, for a companion of fools suffers harm." That verse might sound dramatic, but it's more than advice—it's a spiritual principle. You become like the people you spend the most time with.

That's why I'm writing this letter—not to scare you, but to remind you how important it is to choose your friends with intentionality. You don't need to be afraid of relationships, but you do need to be prayerful and discerning.

As you step into adulthood, people will come in and out of your life. Some will stay for years, others only for a season. Some will challenge you, support you, and cheer for your growth. Others might use you, distract you, or encourage you to compromise. You don't have to be rude, harsh, or judgmental to anyone. Jesus was a friend of sinners—but He didn't let them influence His identity or mission. You can be kind to everyone, but close to only a few.

One of the hardest things to learn—and I've learned it the hard way—is that not every friendly face is a faithful friend. A real friend isn't just someone who makes you laugh or shares your interests. A real friend tells you the truth when you're off track, stands by you when things get messy, and makes you want to be more like Jesus. They call out the best in you, not the worst. They challenge your character, not just your video game skills. They see who you're becoming—and they support that version of you.

Think about the stories you've heard from the scripture. David had Jonathan—a friend who risked everything to protect him and cheer him on. Their friendship was rooted in loyalty, trust, and shared faith. On the flip side, look at King Rehoboam. He ignored the wisdom of his elders and listened to the reckless advice of his young friends—and it split an entire kingdom (1 Kings 12). Friendships matter.

You're already surrounded by some amazing people. Your academic team, bandmates, esports friends—they've brought joy and camaraderie. But even in those groups, be watchful. Are the people you hang out with encouraging you to grow? Do they speak words of life, or do they tear others down? Do they respect your boundaries and your walk with God, or do they try to convince you that compromise is "no big deal"?

You won't always get it right, and that's okay. Sometimes a friend will seem great at first, but over time, their true character comes out. And sometimes the person you didn't expect will become one of your greatest supports. That's why you have to ask God for discernment. Pray before you build deep connections. And when you notice warning signs—don't ignore them.

Another thing to remember is that you are someone else's friend, too. You have influence. Are you the kind of friend who sharpens others? Proverbs 27:17 says, "As iron sharpens iron, so one person sharpens another." Are you encouraging your friends to walk closer with the Lord? Are you trustworthy, honest, dependable? When people spend time with you, do they leave feeling seen, heard, and uplifted?

Friendship isn't about popularity. It's not about how many people are around you at lunch or who follows you online. Real friendships are built in honest conversations, shared values, and standing beside each other in tough times. The people you laugh with are great—but the ones you can cry with, pray with, and be your full self with? Those are the ones worth keeping.

And don't forget—sometimes, choosing the right friends means walking away from the wrong ones. That's not easy, but it's necessary. You can forgive someone and still recognize that the relationship isn't healthy. You don't need to be cruel—just courageous. You don't need to explain yourself to everyone. You answer to God first.

There will be seasons of loneliness. Times when it feels like no one truly "gets" you or shares your convictions. But I promise you—it's better to walk alone with Jesus than to follow a crowd headed in the wrong direction.

Keep your eyes open for those who love God, live with integrity, and care about you for who you are—not for what you can give them. Invest in people who show up, not just when it's fun or convenient, but when it's hard. Be a friend like that. And ask God to bring those kinds of people into your life.

He will. I've seen Him do it over and over.

You are wise, Caleb. You're thoughtful, grounded, and kind. Don't ever lose that. And don't ever settle for surface-level connections. You were created for something deeper—and the right friends will help bring that out of you.

Choose wisely.

Remember Whose you are and Who you represent.
And don't forget to call your mom. ;)

Letter 6

Guarding Your Heart

Dear Caleb,

One of the most important things you can ever learn—and one of the most difficult to live out——is found in Proverbs 4:23: "Above all else, guard your heart, for everything you do flows from it." (NIV)

It sounds simple, but that one verse holds a lifetime of wisdom. Your heart—your core, your mind, your emotions, your desires—is the command center of your life. And when that heart is left unguarded, it doesn't just affect your thoughts or feelings. It affects your actions, your relationships, your decisions, your future. Everything you do flows from it.

That's why this letter matters so much.

Caleb, the world will not tell you to guard your heart. It will tell you to follow it. To chase every feeling. To trust your emotions. To let your desires lead you. But Jeremiah 17:9 (NIV) reminds us, "The heart is deceitful above all things and beyond cure. Who can understand it?" That's not God trying to be harsh—that's Him telling the truth. Left on their own, our hearts are easily swayed, deeply confused, and quick to wander.

So how do you guard your heart?

You start by knowing what goes in. You can't expect purity to flow out of a heart that's constantly fed by impurity. Be mindful of what you watch, what you listen to, and what you laugh at. The world will package sin in the form of entertainment and say it's harmless—but it's not. Every time you absorb something that mocks holiness, that dulls your spiritual sensitivity, that desensitizes you to what God calls sacred—you're letting down your guard.

That doesn't mean you hide in a bubble or fear every interaction with the world. It means you live aware. You feed your heart with what strengthens you. Scripture, worship, truth, community. These are not just Sunday things—they are your guardrails. They keep you aligned with the One who knows your heart better than you ever will.

Guarding your heart also means protecting your emotions—especially in relationships. You'll encounter people who say the right things, who make you feel seen and valued, but who don't carry the same values. Don't give your heart to someone who isn't chasing after God. Don't trade holiness for temporary affection. You were made for more than emotional rollercoasters or surface-level love.

You may not always be able to avoid heartbreak, but you can be intentional with your boundaries. Physical, emotional, and spiritual. Don't apologize for protecting what's sacred. You don't need to prove your loyalty to someone by lowering your standards. The right people will honor your boundaries, not try to blur them.

I know it's not always easy. Culture screams at you to do the opposite of everything God says. But guarding your heart isn't about missing out—it's about being preserved for what's best. It's about staying spiritually alert so you can walk in God's purpose without distraction or detour.

One of the best ways to guard your heart is to give it fully to the Lord. That's the secret. When your heart is anchored in Christ, other things lose their grip. When you love Him most, you're not easily fooled by counterfeits. When you trust Him first, you're not crushed when other people fail you.

Psalm 119:11 says, "I have hidden your word in my heart that I might not sin against you." Fill your heart with the Word. Let it sink deep into the soil of your thoughts. Scripture doesn't just inform—it transforms. It sharpens your discernment and strengthens your resistance to the lies the world will whisper.

Guarding your heart also means protecting your joy. There will be people who drain you, disappoint you, or distract you from God's peace. There will be moments when fear, insecurity, or comparisons try to steal your contentment. Don't let them. Your heart is too important to be tossed around by every feeling or opinion.

Caleb, you are worth protecting. Your calling is worth guarding. Your heart is worth fighting for.

You've already shown wisdom in how you treat others—how you speak gently, how you lead quietly, how you respect boundaries and carry a sense of steadiness that's rare for someone your age. Keep that. Grow in that. And trust that as you guard your heart, God will guard your path.

This won't make you perfect—but it will make you strong. Strong in character. Strong in faith. Strong in conviction. And I promise you, that kind of strength will carry you through every season ahead.

So don't follow your heart—lead it. Don't give it away lightly—entrust it to the One who made it. And don't lower your standards—raise them. Because your life flows from your heart, and your heart belongs to God.

Remember Whose you are and Who you represent.
And don't forget to call your mom. ;)

Letter 7

Integrity in the Small Things

Dear Caleb,

There's a quote I've always loved: "Character is who you are when no one's watching." And Caleb, who you are in the quiet moments—the moments when no one else sees, when no one's grading you, praising you, or holding you accountable—that's the real you.

The world will try to measure success by achievement: grades, awards, popularity, promotions. But God measures something far more lasting: integrity. And integrity starts with the small things.

Luke 16:10 (NIV) says, "Whoever can be trusted with very little can also be trusted with much." This isn't just a proverb—it's a principle of life. If you can be faithful in the unnoticed places, God will entrust you with more. Not because you're perfect, but because you're dependable. Steady. Honest. Whole.

You'll be tempted, as everyone is, to cut corners. To take the easier route when no one's looking. Maybe you'll feel the pull to cheat just a little on an assignment. To tell a half-truth because it's more convenient. To leave a task unfinished because it "doesn't really matter." But I want you to hear me clearly—it always matters.

What you do when no one's watching builds the foundation of your life. Every small decision is a brick. One day, people will look at the house you've built—your reputation, your relationships, your influence—but they won't see the bricks beneath the surface. God sees every single one, and He'll know which ones were placed with honesty, humility, and faithfulness—and which ones were placed with shortcuts and compromise.

Being a man of integrity won't always feel glamorous. In fact, sometimes it will feel lonely. It might even cost you something—a grade, a friendship, an opportunity. But what you gain is worth infinitely more: peace of mind, a clear conscience, and the confidence that you are walking upright before the Lord.

I've seen firsthand how integrity opens doors, and how the lack of it slams them shut. I've watched people get ahead by pretending, only to crumble under pressure later because their character couldn't hold the weight of their success. And I've also watched people—quiet, faithful, honest people—be trusted with more than they ever imagined, simply because they could be trusted in the little things.

You are already a young man who thinks deeply. You weigh your words, care about others, and make choices with intention. That is rare, and it is beautiful. But integrity isn't something you just have once and keep forever. It's something you choose over and over again, when it's hard, when no one notices, and when it costs you.

One of the things I respect most about your dad is his integrity. He doesn't boast. He doesn't pretend to be someone he's not. He just shows up, works hard, and does what's right—even when it's inconvenient or unacknowledged. He's taught me more about faithfulness by his quiet consistency than a thousand sermons could. I pray you carry that same spirit, and I believe you already do.

Integrity will also protect your witness. You can't control what people say about you, but you can control whether it's true. When your words and your actions match, people trust you. When you're honest even when it's hard, people respect you. And when you admit mistakes with humility, people see Christ in you.

Because here's the truth: we all mess up. Integrity isn't about being perfect. It's about being authentic. When you fail—and you will—own it. Ask for forgiveness. Make it right. And then keep walking forward. God doesn't expect you to never stumble. He expects you to be humble enough to stand back up.

In your future career, your friendships, your relationships, and even in your faith, there will always be little choices that test your character. You may never get caught if you lie. No one may ever notice if you slack off. But you will know. And God will know. And your integrity—or lack of it—will either build your future or quietly erode it from the inside out.

You have what it takes to walk in integrity, Caleb. It's not about being the loudest or the most impressive. It's about doing the right thing because it's the right thing. Period. Even when it's hard. Even when no one claps for you. Even when it feels like no one sees.

God sees.

And the people who matter? They see too.

So, choose well in the small things, my son. Because those are the things that become everything.

Remember Whose you are and Who you represent.
And don't forget to call your mom. ;)

Letter 8

Living with Purpose

Dear Caleb,

You were never meant to simply exist. You were created on purpose, for a purpose. Long before you were born, God had already written your name into the pages of His greater story. He knit you together with care, gave you your brilliant mind, your soft heart, your sense of humor, and your love for learning and helping others—none of it by accident.

But here's the thing: purpose isn't always loud. It doesn't always show up in giant moments or public platforms. In fact, most of the time, purpose is lived out in the everyday—in the choices you make, the people you love, the kindness you show, and the way you reflect Christ in even the smallest things.

Colossians 3:23 (NIV) says, "Whatever you do, work at it with all your heart, as working for the Lord, not for human masters." That means whether you're helping a classmate with math, editing a video for a school project, cleaning up after dinner, or pursuing a future career—it all matters. It's all part of your purpose when it's done with the right heart and for the right reasons.

Don't wait for "someday" to start living with purpose. It doesn't begin after graduation, or when you land your first job, or when you check off some big milestone. Purpose begins now. It's woven into how you treat others, how you respond to challenges, how you handle success and failure. It's how you carry the name of Christ in your daily life.

You don't have to know all the details of your future to walk in purpose today. In fact, sometimes the pressure to "figure it all out" becomes a distraction from the very purpose God is unfolding right in front of you. The truth is, your calling isn't just a career, it's a posture. It's being available. Obedient. Willing to say yes to the next right thing.

I believe with all my heart that you're called to impact lives—not just because you're gifted, but because you're grounded. You care about people. You lead with humility. You don't seek attention, but you show up with quiet strength, and that kind of presence is rare and powerful. It's not flashy, it's faithful. And that's exactly the kind of person God loves to use.

Sometimes purpose looks like standing firm when everyone else is going the other way. Sometimes it looks like speaking up when it would be easier to stay quiet. And sometimes, it just means being faithful in the mundane. Showing up and doing your best, even when it feels unnoticed.

Please don't believe the lie that your purpose has to be something huge to be significant. You don't have to change the whole world—just be faithful to change the little corner God has entrusted to you. And when you do that consistently, with love and humility, you're walking in His purpose whether the world notices or not.

There will be times when you question whether you're making a difference. There will be seasons of waiting, confusion, maybe even detours. But hear me—God never wastes anything. Not your waiting. Not your wondering. Not even your wounds. He uses it all.

Ephesians 2:10 (NIV) says, "For we are God's handiwork, created in Christ Jesus to do good works, which God prepared in advance for us to do." That means you don't have to invent your purpose—just step into it. One day at a time. One decision at a time. With your eyes on Jesus and your heart open to His direction.

Be a man who lives intentionally. Who doesn't settle for drifting or going with the crowd. Be someone who asks, "What does God want from my life?" and then actually listens for the answer. Spend time with Him. Read His Word. Talk to Him like the Father He is. Let Him shape your vision and your steps.

You may not always feel like your life is significant—but feelings lie. God doesn't. If He created you, then your life is significant. And if He's leading you, then you can walk boldly into whatever comes next, knowing that your purpose isn't about perfection—it's about faithfulness.

And don't worry, you're not walking into your purpose alone. You have people who believe in you, cheer for you, and pray for you every single day. And most importantly, you have a God who goes before you, walks beside you, and holds your future in His hands.

You were made for more than just fitting in. You were made to shine—not for your own glory, but for His. So live like it. Dream big. Stay humble. Walk with purpose.

Remember Whose you are and Who you represent.
And don't forget to call your mom. ;)

Letter 9

Becoming a Man of Prayer

Dear Caleb,

If I could only teach you one habit that would shape your entire life, it would be prayer.

Not because it's a religious ritual. Not because it's something "good Christians" are supposed to do. But because prayer is the lifeline that connects you to the God who made you, knows you, loves you, and walks with you through every moment of your life.

Prayer is where strength is restored.
Where confusion meets clarity.
Where fear bows to peace.
Where pride gives way to humility.
Where heaven touches earth—and your heart aligns with God's.

It's not just a list of requests. It's a relationship. A rhythm. A refuge.

And Caleb, if you want to be a man of integrity, of purpose, of lasting influence, you must become a man of prayer.

Philippians 4:6–7 (NIV) says, "Do not be anxious about anything, but in every situation, by prayer and petition, with thanksgiving, present your requests to God. And the peace of God, which transcends all understanding, will guard your hearts and your minds in Christ Jesus."

Did you catch that? Prayer is not just about what you say. It's about what God does in response—peace that doesn't even make sense, guarding your heart and mind. In a world filled with noise and pressure and endless opinions, that kind of peace is priceless.

You'll face moments in life when you don't know what to do. You'll wrestle with decisions, disappointments, doubts. People will expect answers from you that you don't have. You might feel like you need to perform, produce, or prove something. And in those moments, I want you to remember—you are not alone.

You have access to the King of kings.
Not just on Sundays. Not just in emergencies. But always.

He listens. He responds. He doesn't need polished words. He just wants your honest heart.

Some of the most powerful prayers you'll ever pray won't be long or eloquent. They'll be whispered in desperation. Mumbled through tears. Offered in silence. And God hears every one of them.

Jesus, who was fully God and fully man, prayed constantly. Before miracles. In moments of joy. In agony in the garden. On the cross. If He needed prayer to stay connected to the Father, how much more do we?

Being a man of prayer doesn't mean you always feel spiritual. It means you build the habit anyway—especially when you don't feel like it. That's how faith grows. That's how your roots deepen. That's how you learn to hear God's voice in a world that's always shouting.

Make time every day—even just a few minutes—to pause and talk to God. Not out of obligation, but out of relationship. Tell Him what's on your mind. Thank Him for what

He's doing. Ask Him for wisdom. Confess when you mess up. Sit in stillness and let Him speak.

You don't need fancy words. You don't need to be in church or on your knees. Sometimes the most sacred moments happen behind the wheel, in your room, or walking between classes. God isn't looking for performance. He's looking for presence.

I've prayed for you since before you were born. And I'll keep praying for you for the rest of my life. But I want you to know how to carry that relationship for yourself. Because one day, you'll be the one interceding for your future wife. Your children. Your friends. Your students. And the prayers you sow now will become the harvest others reap later.

There's a quote I love that says, "You can do more than pray after you've prayed, but you cannot do more than pray until you've prayed." Never forget the power of going to God first—not as a last resort, but as your first response.

Prayer is your strength. Your anchor. Your compass. Your covering.

Be the man who doesn't just talk about God—but talks to Him. Be the man who prays in secret and trusts God in the open. Be the man who isn't ashamed to kneel, to weep, to wrestle, to rejoice—all in the presence of the One who already knows your heart.

Caleb, I see the quiet strength in you. The wisdom beyond your years. The sensitivity that the world may overlook, but that God treasures. I believe you will grow into a man who others turn to for peace, for wisdom, for truth. And that kind of man is shaped in the secret place of prayer.

Keep your Bible open and your heart tender. God will meet you there.

Remember Whose you are and Who you represent.
And don't forget to call your mom. ;)

Letter 10

Courage to Stand Alone

Dear Caleb,

You've heard me say it before: Doing what's right isn't always easy. And I wish I could tell you that life will always reward good choices, that standing for truth will always earn applause, and that living for Jesus will always make you popular. But the truth is: there will be moments when following Christ means standing alone.

And I need you to be ready for that.

Because I believe you're called to be a leader—not just in title, but in the way that really counts. In the quiet choices. In the convictions that cost you something. In the courage to be different.

Daniel knew what that felt like. He was taken from his home, placed in a foreign culture that tried to strip him of his identity, and still, he stood firm. When the king's food was offered, Daniel chose God's way instead. When praying became illegal, Daniel opened his windows and did it anyway (Daniel 6). He didn't start a protest or draw attention to himself. He just lived with quiet courage, and God honored that.

You may not face lions or foreign kings, but you will face pressure.

Pressure to go with the crowd.
Pressure to laugh at things that grieve God.
Pressure to compromise your convictions just a little to fit in.
Pressure to stay silent when you know you should speak up.

It may come in a classroom, in a conversation with friends, on social media, or even in a relationship. And in that moment, you'll have a choice: blend in or stand out.

And standing out? It's lonely sometimes. But hear me—it's worth it.

Romans 12:2 (NIV) says, "Do not conform to the pattern of this world, but be transformed by the renewing of your mind." The world will always offer shortcuts to acceptance. But transformation only happens when you're willing to be different.

And here's the beautiful part: when you stand for what's right, you're never truly alone.

Shadrach, Meshach, and Abednego stood alone before a king who demanded their worship —and when they were thrown into the fire for refusing, guess who showed up? A fourth man in the flames. Jesus Himself. (Daniel 3 KJV)

Caleb, you will never walk into a fiery moment without Jesus walking in with you.

I know you. I've watched you think before you speak, choose kindness over popularity, stay calm when others panic, and quietly hold to your values. That's courage. That's leadership. That's standing when others sit.

And the truth is, there's strength in being willing to be alone—because it shows you know who you are. You're not defined by the crowd. You're grounded in something deeper. You carry truth in your bones. And when you know Who you belong to, you can stand—even if no one else stands with you.

Let me be honest—it still hurts when you're misunderstood. When people question your motives. When you feel excluded. I've been there. Your dad's been there. But those moments have refined us more than any amount of comfort ever could.

Sometimes the stand you take will inspire others to rise up too. Sometimes it won't, and you'll have to trust that obedience is enough, even if no one notices. God sees. And He honors the heart that says, "Even if no one goes with me, I'll still follow You."

Caleb, I pray you always have people in your life who walk the narrow road with you. But when they're not there—when the room feels quiet, and the spotlight is uncomfortable—I pray you walk it anyway. Because truth doesn't change based on who agrees with it. And your convictions don't need permission to matter.

You will face situations that test what you believe. Some will be obvious. Others will be subtle. That's why it's so important to decide now who you are and what you stand for—before the pressure hits. Set your foundation in Christ. Know your values. Hide the Word in your heart. That's what will hold you steady when the winds blow.

Being brave doesn't mean you never feel afraid. It means you do the right thing anyway. And you, my son, have that kind of bravery.

You've already shown it in quiet ways. In the way you lead with humility. In how you treat others with respect, even when they don't return it. In how you've carried faith through difficult seasons, and held tightly to kindness when bitterness could have been easier.

You don't have to be loud to be bold. You don't have to be flashy to be faithful. You just have to stand—one decision at a time, one moment at a time—trusting that God will do the rest.

So stand tall. Stand true. Stand in grace. Stand in truth.

And know that wherever you stand for Christ—He is standing with you.

Remember Whose you are and Who you represent.
And don't forget to call your mom. ;)

Letter 11

When You Fall Short—Grace After Failure

Dear Caleb,

I wish I could promise you that you'll always get it right. That your plans will always succeed, your choices will always be wise, and your intentions will always lead to perfect outcomes. But I can't—because you're human. You're going to fall short sometimes. And that's okay.

This letter isn't about failure. It's about what you do after it.

One of the greatest gifts God has given us is grace. Not grace as a license to mess up, but grace as a lifeline when we do. Romans 5:20 says, "But where sin increased, grace increased all the more." That doesn't mean we take advantage of grace—it means we don't have to be afraid of our shortcomings. Because when we bring them to Jesus, we find forgiveness, not condemnation.

You'll have moments when you say the wrong thing. When you make a decision you wish you could take back. When you look in the mirror and feel like you've disappointed yourself—or worse, disappointed God. In those moments, the enemy will whisper shame. He'll tell you you've ruined it. That you're not good enough. That God's done with you.

But let me tell you the truth: God never walks away from His children.

Not when they fall. Not when they're broken. Not when they mess up.

Psalm 103:12 says, "As far as the east is from the west, so far has he removed our transgressions from us."

That's how completely He forgives you.

The question isn't if you'll fall. It's how you'll respond when you do.

Don't run from God—run to Him. Don't hide—be honest. He's not surprised by your failures. He's not shocked by your sin. He loves you right in the middle of your mess. And when you come to Him with a repentant heart, He restores what was broken. He doesn't just forgive—He rebuilds.

I've failed more times than I can count. But God has never left me. His grace has picked me up again and again. And I've learned that sometimes, failure is the soil where the deepest growth takes root. It humbles you. It teaches you. It draws you closer to the One who never fails.

So, Caleb, when you fall short—and you will—don't stay there. Get back up. Own your mistakes. Make it right when you need to. Learn from it. And let God use it to shape you.

And just as important—extend grace to others when they fall short, too. Don't forget how much grace you've received. Be the kind of man who lifts others up, who doesn't define people by their worst moments, who believes in redemption because he's lived it himself.

Your value isn't based on your performance. It's based on the cross. And Jesus didn't die for the perfect version of you—He died for the real you. The one who needs grace, every day.

So walk in that grace. And offer it freely.
Remember Whose you are and Who you represent.
And don't forget to call your mom. ;)

Letter 12

Handling Temptation and Choosing What's Right

Dear Caleb,

Temptation doesn't come wearing a warning label.
It doesn't announce itself with flashing lights or sirens.
It often looks harmless. Feels justified. Seems small.

But temptation is never about just that one moment—it's about what comes after it.

Jesus knew temptation firsthand. He faced it in the wilderness after fasting for forty days (Matthew 4). The enemy tried to twist truth, appeal to His hunger, His pride, His purpose. But Jesus didn't fight back with willpower—He fought back with the Word. "It is written..." was His weapon of choice. And it's yours, too.

Caleb, you will face temptation—not just once, but often. Temptation to lie to save face. To look at something you shouldn't. To let your anger justify unkindness. To take a shortcut when no one's watching. To say "yes" when your spirit is saying "no." In those moments, I want you to remember: you're not powerless.

1 Corinthians 10:13 (NIV) says, "No temptation has overtaken you except what is common to mankind. And God is faithful; He will not let you be tempted beyond what

you can bear." That means every time temptation shows up, God provides away out. You just have to look for it—and choose it.

It won't always feel easy. Doing the right thing sometimes costs you something. You might lose a friend, feel embarrassed, miss out on something everyone else is doing. But obedience to God is never wasted. The momentary discomfort of saying "no" is nothing compared to the peace that comes from living with integrity.

And when you do resist temptation—celebrate that! Not in pride, but in gratitude. Every time you say no to sin and yes to holiness, you're becoming stronger. You're training your heart to choose what honors God, even when it's hard.

But I also need you to know this: if you slip—if you give in—that doesn't disqualify you. God isn't done with you when you fall. But don't normalize it. Don't numb your conscience. Bring it into the light. Repent quickly. Let God heal what was cracked. And let that moment remind you of how much you need His strength.

Temptation often grows in isolation. So don't try to fight it alone. Surround yourself with people who speak truth, not just comfort. People who will hold you accountable because they love you. You don't have to be perfect, but you do need to be real.

And Caleb, be careful what you feed your mind and your heart. What you watch, listen to, scroll through, and laugh at—it all forms a path. And that path either leads you closer to Christ or slowly, quietly pulls you away. Guard it fiercely.

You are not weak for being tempted. Even Jesus was tempted. You are only defeated if you choose to stay there. But you are filled with the Spirit of God—the same Spirit that raised Jesus from the dead (Romans 8:11). And with His power, you can walk away from temptation and into the freedom that comes with obedience.

So, when temptation whispers—don't listen. Walk away. Run if you have to. And let every "no" to sin be a "yes" to the life God has for you.

You were made for more.

Remember Whose you are and Who you represent.
And don't forget to call your mom. ;)

Letter 13

Stewardship—Money, Time, and Responsibility

Dear Caleb,

One of the clearest signs of maturity isn't just what you believe—it's what you do with what you've been given. That's called stewardship.

You may not hear that word often outside of church, but it's a concept that shows up everywhere in life. Stewardship is simply managing well what God has entrusted to you—your money, your time, your gifts, your opportunities, your relationships. It's recognizing that none of it really belongs to you, but you're responsible for how you use it.

Psalm 24:1 (NIV) says, "The earth is the Lord's, and everything in it, the world, and all who live in it." That means everything you "own"—your income, your schedule, your talents—is actually on loan from God. And how you handle those things reflects your heart.

Let's start with money. I know it's a topic most people either obsess over or avoid. But how you handle money will shape your future, your peace of mind, and even your ability to be generous. Proverbs 21:5 (NIV) says, "The plans of the diligent lead to profit as surely as haste leads to poverty." That means budgeting, planning, saving—those aren't just smart moves, they're biblical ones.

Tithe your first fruits. Give back to God before you spend on yourself. Not because He needs your money, but because giving reminds your heart Who's in charge. Save steadily, spend wisely, and avoid the trap of debt whenever possible. And don't forget—generosity isn't about how much you have, it's about how open your hands are. Whether you're giving $5 or $500, God sees the heart behind it.

Now let's talk about time. You only get 24 hours in a day—and every single one of them is a gift. Ephesians 5:15-16a (NIV) tells us to "Be very careful, then, how you live—not as unwise but as wise, making the most of every opportunity." Time is something you can never get back. Once it's spent, it's gone. Use it on things that matter. Prioritize people over screens. Rest, but don't be lazy. Work hard, but don't let busyness become your identity. Know when to say "yes" and when to say "no."

Your time will either serve your purpose or sabotage it. Make your calendar reflect your values.

And lastly—responsibility. Being a good steward means taking ownership, even when it's hard. Show up when you say you will. Do your best, even when no one is checking. Admit your mistakes and make them right. Whether you're leading a group, doing chores, working a job, or helping a friend—do it as if you're doing it for the Lord. (Colossians 3:23)

Don't wait for someone to hand you authority. Steward well what you already have, and God will increase it.

Caleb, you are already such a thoughtful, reliable young man. I've watched you serve others, take initiative, and follow through with excellence. You may not always feel like you're making a difference, but stewardship is about the long game. You're building something solid, and God honors that.

This isn't about perfection. It's about faithfulness. And every time you choose to handle what you've been given with care, wisdom, and integrity, you're saying to God, "I'm ready for more."

Be a good steward. Of your money. Your time. Your influence. Your gifts. Your relationships. Your character. Handle what you've been given with open hands and a faithful heart and watch what God will do.

Remember Whose you are and Who you represent.
And don't forget to call your mom. ;)

Letter 14

Honoring Women and Building Godly Relationships

Dear Caleb,

One day, you may fall in love. Maybe you already have. Whether that happens tomorrow or years from now, this letter is about how you treat others—especially women—not just in dating, but in friendship, conversation, and everyday life.

The world has a lot to say about relationships. It tells you to follow your feelings, chase chemistry, and put yourself first. It normalizes using people, ghosting them, crossing boundaries, and calling it "freedom." But God calls us to something radically different—honor.

Romans12:10 (NIV) says, "Be devoted to one another in love. Honor one another above yourselves."

That's where true relationships begin—not in attraction, but in honor.

Honoring a woman means seeing her as someone created in the image of God—not someone to impress, pursue for selfish reasons, or conquer emotionally or physically. It means respecting her boundaries, her worth, her thoughts, and her walk with Christ. Whether she's a classmate, a friend, or someone you one day fall in love with, treat her like someone Jesus died for—because she is.

I've prayed for the girl you'll one day date or marry. I've prayed she loves Jesus, speaks truth, laughs with joy, and stands firm in who she is. And I've prayed that you would be the kind of man who makes her feel safe, supported, challenged, and cherished.

Physical boundaries matter. Not because your body is bad, but because it's sacred. God created physical attraction—but He also created covenant. Save intimacy for the relationship He designed it for: marriage. Not out of shame, but out of reverence. Out of a desire to give your future wife the gift of restraint, not regret.

And if you ever slip or make a mistake, don't hide in shame—run to Jesus. His grace covers your past, and His Spirit empowers your future.

You also honor women by the way you talk—not just to them, but about them. The jokes you laugh at, the media you consume, the conversations you entertain—they shape your heart. Don't normalize disrespect. Don't speak about women in ways that cheapen their worth or reduce them to objects. Be the man in the room who raises the standard.

And remember—Godly relationships aren't just about compatibility. They're about shared purpose. The right relationship will point you both closer to Christ, not pull you farther away. Don't compromise on that. I know it might feel like "asking too much," but I promise you this—it's worth the wait.

Look for someone who challenges you spiritually. Who prays with you. Who speaks truth when it's uncomfortable. Who lives with conviction and joy. And be that kind of person in return. The best relationships aren't built on perfection—they're built on two people committed to growing in grace, honesty, and faithfulness together.

And if you're ever unsure what love looks like, just open your Bible to 1 Corinthians 13: "Love is patient, love is kind... It does not dishonor others... It is not self-seeking... It always protects, always trusts, always hopes, always perseveres."

That's the standard. Not movies. Not social media. Not your friends. The Word of God.

Whether you're in a relationship now or years down the road, I want you to walk with integrity. To guard your heart and hers. To build something beautiful—something holy—brick by brick, with truth and trust and time.

Because the way you treat women says a lot about your walk with God.

So be gentle. Be honest. Be strong. Be kind. And don't settle for anything less than a love that honors God.

Remember Whose you are and Who you represent.
And don't forget to call your mom. ;)

Letter 15

Living as a Servant Leader

Dear Caleb,

The world will try to tell you that leadership is about titles, applause, control, and being the one out front. But Jesus turned that idea upside down.

In Matthew 20:26–28 (NIV), Jesus said, "Whoever wants to become great among you must be your servant… just as the Son of Man did not come to be served, but to serve, and to give his life as a ransom for many."

Real leadership isn't about being in charge.
It's about choosing to serve—even when you don't have to.

Caleb, I see leadership in you already. In your quiet strength. In the way you notice the needs of others. In how people trust you to show up, follow through, and speak truth gently. That kind of leadership doesn't always get the spotlight—but it changes lives.

Servant leadership means putting others first—not to be walked on, but to lift others up. It means asking, "How can I help?" instead of, "What's in it for me?" It means showing up early, staying late, and doing the unseen things no one else wants to do—not for credit, but because it's right. Your dad lives this daily. Watch him closely.

Jesus, the King of Kings, knelt to wash His disciples' feet. That act wasn't weakness; it was divine strength. And that's your model.

Leadership doesn't mean being perfect. It means being responsible. It means owning your decisions, admitting when you're wrong, and choosing humility over pride. It means seeing people as valuable, not as tools to get things done.

In school, work, ministry, and even in your own future family, you'll have opportunities to lead. Don't wait for authority to be handed to you. Lead where you are. Set the tone. Treat others with respect. Invite people in. Encourage more than you criticize. Protect the vulnerable. Celebrate others' wins. Be the thermostat, not the thermometer.

And when people follow you—point them to Christ, not to yourself.

You don't need a stage to lead. You just need a heart that beats like Jesus.
And Caleb, you have that heart.

I pray you always lead with love. That you value character over charisma. That you stay teachable, no matter how high you rise. That you never stop asking God, "How can I serve the people you've placed in my life today?"

That's the kind of leader the world needs.

That's the kind of leader you already are becoming.

Remember Whose you are and Who you represent.
And don't forget to call your mom. ;)

Letter 16

Finding Your Identity in a World That Labels You

Dear Caleb,

This world will try to name you.

It will slap labels on you based on your accomplishments, your personality, your failures, your appearance, your grades, your opinions, your relationships—and sometimes even your past. It will try to define you by the surface and ignore the soul underneath. But I want you to hear this clearly:

The only name that truly defines you is the one God gave you—His.

You are His workmanship (Ephesians 2:10).
You are a child of God (John 1:12).
You are chosen, not forsaken (1 Peter 2:9).
You are redeemed (Ephesians 1:7).
You are called (2 Timothy 1:9).
You are deeply loved (Romans 8:38–39).

This world loves boxes. It wants to categorize you, package you, and make your worth dependent on how well you fit in. But you were never meant to fit in. You were meant to stand out—not for attention, but for truth.

Your identity isn't in your performance. Not in the awards you win or the goals you hit. It's not in your friendships, your failures, or how many likes you get on social media. It's not even in how others see you—it's in how God sees you.

And God sees you as His.

When you were a little boy, I saw glimpses of this strong identity forming. You always had a quiet confidence—not arrogance, but assurance. You didn't need the crowd to validate you. You didn't chase attention. That is rare. And I pray you carry that with you forever.

Because the older you get, the louder the noise becomes. There will be people who misunderstand you. Who try to put you in a box that doesn't fit. Who expect you to be something you're not. Don't let them shrink who you are to make themselves feel more comfortable. You were never meant to live small.

But here's the key: your identity in Christ doesn't make you proud. It makes you secure. You don't need to prove yourself to anyone when you know that you're already approved by the God who made you. You can walk into any room with confidence, because you carry the Spirit of the Living God within you.

Knowing who you are in Christ frees you to love others—even the ones who label you. It allows you to forgive when people misunderstand or misjudge you. It gives you peace when life gets confusing. And it reminds you that your worth is fixed—no matter what you face.

So, when the world tries to name you—pause. Go to the Word. Ask, "God, what do You call me?" And then walk in that.

Because you are not your GPA.
You are not your setbacks.
You are not your status.
You are not your fears.

You are not who others say you are.

You are who He says you are.

And that truth will carry you further than anything else in this life.

Remember Whose you are and Who you represent.
And don't forget to call your mom. ;)

Letter 17

Choosing Humility Over Pride

Dear Caleb,

You have so many reasons to be proud—your intelligence, your accomplishments, your heart for others, your leadership, your character. But today I want to talk to you about something far more powerful than pride: humility.

The world celebrates pride. It says, "Show off your success. Prove your worth. Be the loudest voice in the room." But God says something very different: "God opposes the proud but shows favor to the humble." (James 4:6, NIV)

Pride seeks attention. Humility seeks to serve.
Pride says, "Look at me." Humility says, "How can I lift someone else?"
Pride craves control. Humility surrenders to God's will.

Humility isn't weakness—it's strength under control. Jesus, the Savior of the world, knelt to wash His disciples' feet. He deserved to be served, but He chose to serve. That's what real greatness looks like.

Caleb, people will notice your gifts. They'll affirm your leadership. And you'll likely find yourself in positions of influence. When that happens—and it will—don't let it go to your head. Let it go to your heart. Ask God, "How can I use this for Your glory, not mine?"

Be the kind of man who doesn't need to be the center of attention to feel valuable. Be the one who notices when someone's left out. Who holds the door. Who says thank you. Who admits when he's wrong. Who gives others credit. Who listens more than he speaks. Those things may not make headlines—but they reflect the heart of Jesus.

Humility also protects you from comparison. When you're secure in who God made you to be, you don't have to measure yourself against anyone else. You can celebrate others without feeling threatened. You can walk into a room without needing to prove anything. That kind of peace is powerful—and rare.

Pride whispers, "You've earned this." Humility says, "Everything I have is a gift." And, Caleb, everything you are and everything you do is by the grace of God. You've worked hard, yes—but your breath, your mind, your talents, your opportunities—they're all from Him.

Don't ever be afraid to take the low place. God has a way of lifting up those who don't lift themselves.

Luke 14:11 (NIV) says, "For all those who exalt themselves will be humbled, and those who humble themselves will be exalted."

I've seen you choose humility already. In the way you treat your peers. In how you help without needing recognition. In how you quietly lead by example. Keep that heart, Caleb. It will open more doors than pride ever could—and it will keep your character strong when those doors open.

So stay grounded. Stay teachable. Stay close to the Lord. And remember—the most powerful man in history wore a crown of thorns and carried a towel.

That's who we follow.

Remember Whose you are and Who you represent.

And don't forget to call your mom. ;)

Letter 18

Dealing with Disappointment and Delayed Dreams

Dear Caleb,

There's something no one really prepares you for when you're young, the sting of disappointment.

You grow up dreaming big. You make plans. You put in the work. You hope with your whole heart. But sometimes… it still doesn't turn out like you imagined.

The acceptance letter doesn't come.
The opportunity falls through.
The person you counted on walks away.
The thing you prayed for feels unanswered.

And you're left wondering: Why, God? Why did You or didn't You let this happen?

I've wrestled with that same question. I've sat in the silence, felt the ache, and begged God to change the outcome. Sometimes He has. Sometimes He hasn't. But in every single case, I've learned this truth—God's "no" or "not yet" is never without purpose. My dad recently reminded me to not ask why I am going through something, but to ask God what He wants me to learn through it. Beyond that, ask Him to show you how to give Him glory through it.

Proverbs16:9 (NIV) says, "In their hearts humans plan their course, but the Lord establishes their steps." That means even when your plans shift, your purpose doesn't.

Disappointment is hard because it makes you feel out of control. It reminds you that you're not in charge—and that's actually a gift. Because when your dreams don't come true on your timeline, it gives space for God's dreams to take root.

Delayed doesn't mean denied.
And even when God closes a door, He opens something better—not always easier, but better in ways you might not see right away.

Caleb, you are allowed to grieve what didn't happen. You don't have to pretend you're okay. God can handle your disappointment. He doesn't shame you for feeling let down. He meets you there—and gently lifts your eyes back to Him.

Don't let disappointment harden your heart. Let it deepen your faith.

Because here's what I know: your story isn't on pause. It's being written—in valleys and victories, in waiting and wondering. God is always working behind the scenes, weaving things together for your good (Romans 8:28). He's never late, even when it feels like He's forgotten you.

So, what do you do when dreams are delayed?

You keep trusting.
You keep showing up.
You stay faithful in the small things.
You cry when you need to.
You worship anyway.

Because disappointment may visit, but it doesn't get to stay.

And sometimes, years later, you'll look back and thank God for the thing you thought you needed—because His plan was so much greater than what you asked for.

You're not failing when you're discouraged—you're growing. And those growing seasons produce the strongest roots.

So lift your head, my son. God hasn't forgotten you. He's preparing you.

And your story? It's not finished yet.

Remember Whose you are and Who you represent.
And don't forget to call your mom. ;)

Letter 19

Being a Light in a Dark World

Dear Caleb,

You don't have to look far to see that the world can be a heavy, hurting, and dark place.

There's confusion, division, injustice, fear, anger, loneliness. People are searching for hope in all the wrong places. They're desperate to be seen, loved, and rescued—even when they don't know how to say it.

And that's why your life matters so much.

Because Jesus didn't call us to hide from the darkness—He called us to shine in the middle of it.

Matthew 5:14–16 (NIV) says,
"You are the light of the world. A town built on a hill cannot be hidden… Let your light shine before others, that they may see your good deeds and glorify your Father in heaven."

That's not just a beautiful verse, it's a mission.

Caleb, the world doesn't need more people blending in. It needs more people willing to shine—not for attention, but for impact. That means you choose joy when it's easier to complain. You show kindness when others are cold. You speak truth when the crowd stays silent. You love with patience, humility, and grace.

And you do it not because people deserve it, but because Jesus has done it for you.

Being a light doesn't mean you have all the answers. It means you know where the answers are found. It means your life points to something—Someone—greater.

Sometimes, shining your light will inspire others. Sometimes, it'll make you feel misunderstood or even rejected. That's okay. Don't dim your light just to make others comfortable. Shine anyway. You never know who's watching—and who might find hope through your courage.

You can be bold and gentle at the same time. Strong and kind. Convicted and compassionate. In fact, that's exactly how Jesus lived. He didn't compromise truth, and He didn't hold back love. He walked in both—and we're called to do the same.

In your school, your friendships, your future workplace, your future family—be the one who brings light. That doesn't mean being perfect. It means being present. It means choosing holiness in a culture of compromise. It means carrying the peace of God wherever you go.

And remember—light doesn't have to fight darkness. It just has to show up.

The darker the world gets, the brighter your light will shine.

And Caleb, your light is strong. Not because of who you are, but because of Who lives in you.

So walk with confidence. Speak with love. And keep shining—even when it feels like no one notices.

Because someone will. And more importantly, God sees every flicker of faith.

Remember Whose you are and Who you represent.
And don't forget to call your mom. ;)

Letter 20

Living for an Audience of One

Dear Caleb,

There will always be people watching you.

Some will admire you.
Some will misunderstand you.
Some will expect too much.
Some will criticize no matter what you do.

And if you're not careful, you'll start performing—shaping your words, your decisions, even your dreams to gain approval from people who were never meant to define your worth.

That's why I want you to remember this:
You were never called to live for the crowd. You were called to live for Christ.

Galatians 1:10 (NIV) asks, "Am I now trying to win the approval of human beings, or of God? Or am I trying to please people? If I were still trying to please people, I would not be a servant of Christ."

You can't live for both—because eventually, the two paths will pull in opposite directions.

There will be times when obedience to God means disappointing others. When standing for truth means being left out. When doing the right thing means missing out on something the world celebrates. And in those moments, I want you to ask: Who am I doing this for?

When you live for the applause of people, your identity rises and falls with their opinions. But when you live for the glory of God, your foundation stays steady—because He never changes.

This world rewards performance. But God sees the heart. He honors the choices no one sees, the prayers no one hears, the kindness you give with no expectation of return. Living for Him doesn't always come with instant praise—but it always comes with eternal reward.

That's what Jesus did. He didn't chase popularity—He followed the Father. He didn't fit in—He changed the world. And at the end of His life, He didn't hear, "You impressed the masses." He heard, "Well done."

That's the only applause that matters.

I want you to dream big, Caleb. I want you to lead, create, influence, and thrive. But more than anything, I want you to live with your eyes fixed on Jesus. Because everything else—the titles, the trophies, the attention—will eventually fade. But what you do for Him will last forever.

When you wake up each day, ask:
"God, how can I honor You today—in what I say, in how I love, in what I choose?"

And when your head hits the pillow, may your peace come not from applause, but from knowing you lived in step with your Savior.

You were made to live bold. Brave. Free.
Not for the approval of man—but for the glory of the One who made you.

That's living for an audience of One.

Remember Whose you are and Who you represent.
And don't forget to call your mom. ;)

Final Blessing and Prayer

Dear Lord,

Thank You for the incredible gift of my son. Thank You for shaping him, guiding him, and calling him to something greater than anything this world could offer. I lift Caleb up to You now—not as someone I want to control or protect forever, but as someone I fully entrust to You.

Go before him, Lord. Walk beside him. Fill him with wisdom beyond his years, courage when he's afraid, and clarity when he's unsure. Let Your Word be a lamp to his feet and a light to his path. Let Your Spirit guide his choices, soften his heart, and strengthen his faith.

May he become a man of integrity, humility, boldness, and compassion. May his life reflect Your grace, his steps follow Your lead, and his heart stay rooted in truth. Help him to know that no matter what the world says, Your voice is the one that matters most.

Thank You for the years I've had with him and ones still to come—and for the legacy You're still writing through his life.

Keep him close, Lord.
And help him always remember—he is loved, he is chosen, and he is Yours.
He is fiercely loved—by me, and even more so by You.

In Jesus' name, Amen.

And please, Lord, remind him to call his mom. ;)

About the author

Amy Tisdale

Amy resides in Oklahoma and is a published author, speaker, and is actively involved in her church. She is a wife, mom, grandma, travel agent, and the 2024-2025 Ms. Wheelchair Oklahoma USA.

Made in the USA
Coppell, TX
03 May 2025

48979350R00046